Introduc

# Keep That Temple Clean: A Biblical Perspective

Jeremy B. Sims

Published by Jeremy Sims, 2023.

KEEP THAT TEMPLE CLEAN: A BIBLICAL PERSPECTIVE

**First edition. November 18, 2023.**

Copyright © 2023 Jeremy B. Sims.

ISBN: 979-8223124344

Written by Jeremy B. Sims.

# Also by Jeremy B. Sims

The phrase "cleanliness is next to godliness" is not directly found in the Bible. However, the sentiment behind this saying resonates deeply with biblical teachings. The Scriptures emphasize the importance of purity, both in the physical and spiritual sense. One can draw connections to the numerous ceremonial cleansings and rites in the Old Testament that symbolize the desire for spiritual purity. These rituals served as a tangible reminder of the need for inner righteousness and the removal of sin, reflecting a deep reverence towards God.

The New Testament deepens this idea by introducing the notion that our bodies are temples of the Holy Spirit. In 1 Corinthians 6:19-20, Paul writes, "Do you not know that your bodies are temples of the Holy Spirit, who is in you, whom you have received from God? You are not your own; you were bought at a price. Therefore, honor God with your bodies." This proclamation elevates the idea of physical cleanliness and purity to spiritual significance. Our bodies are not mere vessels but sacred sites where the Spirit of God resides. This realization should inspire believers to treat their bodies with utmost respect and care, keeping them free from harm and defilement.

Maintaining a clean temple is of particular significance when contemplating the coming of Christ. Believers are instructed to be ready and watchful for the second coming, often described as the bridegroom coming for His bride, the Church. Just as a bride prepares herself, ensuring she is spotless and adorned for her groom, so should believers prepare themselves for Christ. This readiness involves purifying the heart, mind, and body, ensuring they reflect God's holiness. Revelations 19:7-8 describes the Church being ready for the wedding of the Lamb, having made herself clean and adorned in bright linen, symbolizing the righteous acts of God's people.

In essence, the intertwining themes of cleanliness and the body as a temple underscore the sanctity of human life and the profound responsibility believers carry in upholding this sanctity. With the anticipation of Christ's return, the commitment to purity and righteousness becomes not just a discipline but a joyous act of worship, honoring the God who resides within.

# Chapter 1: Understanding the Temple

In ancient times, temples were more than mere structures; they were sacred spaces where the divine intersected with the mundane. These hallowed places where the epicenters of spiritual activity and held profound significance in various cultures, with each temple uniquely tailored to the deity it honored.

For the Israelites, the temple in Jerusalem was the embodiment of God's presence among His people. This was not just a place for rituals; it was where heaven met earth. The temple stood as a testament to God's covenant with Israel and His faithfulness to His promises. Its design, as detailed in the scriptures, emphasized both God's grandeur and His accessibility. The Holy of Holies, the innermost chamber of the temple, housed the Ark of the Covenant and represented God's direct presence. Only the high priest could enter this space, and even then, only once a year on the Day of Atonement. This exclusivity underlined the sanctity of the relationship between God and His people, and the reverence required.

The transition from the Old to the New Testament brings forth a transformative understanding of temples. While the Old Testament focused on the physical temple in Jerusalem, the New Testament introduced a more personal and intimate interpretation. The Apostle Paul, in 1 Corinthians 6:19-20, proclaims, "Do you not know that your bodies are temples of the Holy Spirit, who is in you, whom you have received from God? You are not your own; you were bought at a price. Therefore, honor God with your bodies." Here, Paul is not speaking about a structure of stone and mortar but of the human body. This shift in understanding marks a significant departure from traditional views.

Paul's revelation is revolutionary. It suggests that God's presence is no longer confined to a specific geographic location but dwells within each believer. This democratization of the divine redefines the relationship between God and humans. No longer do people need to journey to a particular place to encounter the divine; the divine resides within, making every act, thought, and decision a potential act of worship or desecration.

Understanding this concept is crucial for believers. If our bodies are indeed temples of the Holy Spirit, then the care, respect, and sanctity we afford to them should mirror the reverence shown to sacred spaces in ancient times. The implications are profound; every action, every decision, and every thought should be approached with the awareness of God's indwelling presence. The temple, thus, transforms from an external structure to an internal sanctum, forever linking the physical with the spiritual in the life of the believer.

## Self-Assessment: Do You Understand Your Temple? Questions to Ponder

**Awareness:** Do you recognize and believe that your body is a temple of the Holy Spirit, as stated in 1 Corinthians 6:19-20?

**Reverence:** How do you show reverence and respect for your body, recognizing it as a sacred space where God dwells?

**Physical Care:** Are you attentive to the needs of your body, ensuring it gets proper nutrition, exercise, and rest?

**Spiritual Nourishment:** How often do you feed your spirit with prayer, meditation, and the study of God's Word?

**Mental Clarity:** What practices have you adopted to ensure your mind remains clear, focused, and free from negative or harmful thoughts?

**Emotional Health:** How do you handle emotional distress or turmoil? Do you seek guidance and healing when faced with emotional wounds?

**Guardianship:** What measures do you take to protect your body, mind, and spirit from negative influences or temptations?

**Sacred Spaces:** Beyond your body, do you maintain other spaces in your life (like your home or workspace) with the same level of reverence and cleanliness?

**Connections:** Do you surround yourself with individuals who respect and understand the sanctity of their temples? How do these relationships influence your personal journey?

**Repentance and Redemption:** When you falter or stray, how do you approach repentance and seek reconciliation with God?

**Purpose and Service:** Recognizing your body as a vessel for God's work, how are you using your talents, skills, and energies to serve Him and others?

**Continuous Growth:** Are you actively seeking knowledge and understanding to better care for your temple and draw closer to God?

**Legacy and Influence:** How do you inspire and encourage others to recognize and honor their bodies as temples?

**Anticipation:** With the understanding that Christ will return, how does this shape your daily choices and long-term goals in caring for your temple?

**Reflection:** Taking a moment of introspection, are there areas in your life where you feel your temple needs renovation, healing, or a deeper connection with God?

By pondering these questions, believers can gain a deeper understanding of how they view and treat their temple. The answers can offer guidance on areas that might need attention, fostering a closer relationship with God and a deeper appreciation for the gift of the Holy Spirit within.

# Chapter 2: The Body as a Vessel

The body's role as a sacred vessel is a recurrent theme throughout the Bible. Its sanctity is not merely a construct of religious doctrine but is grounded in the very scriptures that serve as the foundation for Christian faith.

**Biblical References Highlighting the Body's Sanctity:**

**Creation's Crown**: In Genesis 1:27, we are told, "So God created mankind in his own image, in the image of God he created them; male and female he created them." This passage emphasizes the unique position humans hold in the hierarchy of creation, crafted in the very likeness of the Creator.

**Temples of the Spirit**: As previously mentioned in 1 Corinthians 6:19-20, believers are reminded that their bodies are temples of the Holy Spirit, thereby sanctifying every believer's body.

**Bought with a Price**: Building upon the theme in 1 Corinthians, verse 20 states, "you were bought at a price." This references Christ's sacrifice, reminding believers of the immense value and sanctity of their bodies.

**Members of Christ's Body**: In 1 Corinthians 12:27, Paul states, "Now you are the body of Christ, and each one of you is a part of it." Each believer, therefore, is integrally connected to Christ, further underscoring the body's sanctity.

**Practices and Habits to Keep Our Bodies Pure and Healthy:**

**Dietary Discipline**: Drawing inspiration from scriptures like Daniel 1, where Daniel and his friends chose a diet that honored God, believers can prioritize nutritious and wholesome foods that nourish the body.

**Physical Activity**: In 1 Timothy 4:8, while spiritual discipline holds ultimate importance, there's recognition that "physical training is of some value." Regular exercise and physical activity can be viewed as honoring the body as God's temple.

**Rest and Sabbaths**: The concept of the Sabbath, rooted in Genesis 2:2-3, emphasizes rest's importance. Adequate sleep and regular periods of rest rejuvenate the body and spirit.

**Avoiding Harmful Substances**: Proverbs 20:1 warns about the perils of excessive wine and intoxication. By extension, believers should avoid substances that harm or degrade the body.

**Meditation and Prayer**: Spiritual practices like meditation on God's word (Psalm 1:2) and regular prayer (Philippians 4:6-7) contribute to mental and emotional well-being, harmonizing body and spirit.

**Fellowship**: Regular interaction with a community of believers, as seen in Acts 2:42-47, fosters emotional health and spiritual growth, providing support and accountability.

**Purity**: Abstaining from sexual immorality, as emphasized in 1 Thessalonians 4:3-5, ensures the body remains pure, honoring its role as the Holy Spirit's temple.

**Mindful Consumption**: Beyond food, what one consumes in terms of media, conversations, and literature affects the mind and soul. Philippians 4:8 encourages believers to focus on whatever is pure, lovely, and commendable.

In essence, the body's sanctity isn't a mere theological construct; it demands actionable respect and care. Through mindful practices and habits, believers can honor their bodies, ensuring they remain vessels worthy of the Holy Spirit's indwelling.

## Self-Assessment: Your Body as a Temple - Questions to Ponder

**In His Image:** Do you truly believe and understand that you are made in the image of God, as mentioned in Genesis? How does this belief shape your self-worth and self-image?

**Daily Nutrition:** Are you mindful of what you eat and drink, selecting nourishing foods that sustain and respect the body God has given you?

**Physical Activity:** How often do you engage in physical activity? Do you view exercise as a form of worship or thanksgiving for your health and capabilities?

**Rest and Renewal:** Are you intentional about getting adequate rest, mirroring God's design of Sabbath rest for rejuvenation?

**Toxins and Temptations:** Are there harmful substances or habits you knowingly introduce to your body? What steps could you take to eliminate or reduce them?

**Sexual Purity:** How do you uphold the biblical standard of purity in your relationships and personal life?

**Mental Diet:** What do you "feed" your mind? Are the media, literature, and conversations you engage in edifying and pure?

**Guarding the Heart:** Proverbs 4:23 advises to guard one's heart above all else. How do you shield your heart and emotions from negative influences and harm?

**Holy Interactions:** How do your interactions with others reflect the sanctity of your body as God's temple? Do your words and actions bring honor to Him?

**Spiritual Nourishment:** In what ways do you ensure that your spiritual self is as nourished and healthy as your physical self?

**Purposeful Living:** Considering your body as a vessel for God's work, are there specific callings or missions you feel drawn to? How are you pursuing them?

**Healing and Wholeness:** Are there physical or emotional wounds you carry that need healing? How can you seek God's restoration in these areas?

**Dress and Presentation:** Do you consider your attire and presentation as expressions of respect for your body as God's temple? How do they reflect your understanding of this biblical principle?

**Continuous Growth:** Are there habits or disciplines you'd like to adopt to better honor your body as a temple? What steps can you take to implement them?

**Gratitude:** How often do you express gratitude for the health, capabilities, and life God has granted you?

Reflecting on these questions can provide insight into how closely one's life aligns with the biblical view of the body as a temple. It offers an opportunity for self-awareness, growth, and a deeper commitment to honoring God through one's physical vessel.

# Chapter 3: Cleansing the Mind

The mind, a centerpiece of human consciousness, is where decisions are birthed, beliefs are nurtured, and emotions are processed. However, its intangible nature doesn't make it immune to corruption; in fact, its susceptibility to external influences is immense. A corrupt mind can pave the way for actions that misalign with God's will and our true purpose.

### The Dangers of a Corrupt Mind:

A mind inundated with negative, impure, or harmful thoughts can manifest these perceptions into actions. Such a mind becomes fertile ground for sin, resentment, jealousy, and myriad destructive behaviors. From a behavioral standpoint, consistent negative thinking patterns can spiral into disorders such as anxiety, depression, and even cognitive distortions that skew reality.

### Biblical Advice on Purifying Thoughts:

The Bible, understanding the mind's pivotal role, offers guidance on its purification. Romans 12:2 urges believers not to conform to the world but to be transformed by renewing the mind. This renewal is a continual process of aligning one's thoughts with the will and purpose of God. In 2 Corinthians 10:5, believers are instructed to take captive every thought and make it obedient to Christ. This act of taking thoughts captive signifies an active role in filtering and governing one's thinking processes.

### The Role of Meditation and Reflection on God's Word:

Joshua 1:8 advises, "Keep this Book of the Law always on your lips; meditate on it day and night, so that you may be careful to do everything written in it. Then you will be prosperous and successful." Meditation here isn't the passive act of reflection; it's an active, deliberate rumination on God's Word. This immersion into scripture naturally purifies thoughts by saturating the mind with divine truths. Philippians 4:8 provides a blueprint for the type of thoughts one should entertain:

"Finally, brothers and sisters, whatever is true, whatever is noble, whatever is right, whatever is pure, whatever is lovely, whatever is admirable—if anything is excellent or praiseworthy—think about such things."

## A Ministerial and Holistic Approach with a Human Behaviorist Perspective:

Ministers often emphasize the sanctity of the mind, urging believers to guard and nurture it with the same care as the heart. They advocate for community, accountability, and mentorship to support individuals in their journey to mental purity.

From a behaviorist perspective, the environment plays a crucial role in shaping thought processes. The stimuli one exposes themselves to—be it media, relationships, or daily experiences—can either reinforce or challenge existing beliefs. By understanding this, one can consciously curate environments that promote positive thinking and align with biblical principles. Holistically, incorporating practices such as mindfulness, cognitive-behavioral techniques, and positive reinforcement can aid in guiding the mind towards purity.

In conclusion, cleansing the mind is not a singular act but a continuous journey. By integrating biblical wisdom with holistic and behaviorist insights, believers can equip themselves with a robust toolkit to navigate the challenges of maintaining mental purity in an increasingly complex world.

## Self-Assessment on Cleansing the Mind for an Adult:

**Thought Patterns:** What dominant thoughts occupy your mind daily? Are they mostly positive, negative, or neutral?

**Scripture Engagement:** How frequently do you meditate on scripture or spiritual teachings?

**Media Consumption:** What type of content (books, movies, news) do you consume regularly? Does it uplift or deplete your spirit?

**Mindfulness:** How often do you practice mindfulness or intentional reflection?

**External Influences:** Are there external environments or relationships that consistently lead you to negative or harmful thoughts?

**Active Renewal:** How do you actively combat intrusive or negative thoughts?

**Self-Talk:** How do you speak to yourself mentally, especially after making mistakes or facing challenges?

**Professional Assistance:** Have you considered or sought professional guidance, like counseling or therapy, to address persistent negative thought patterns?

**Daily Habits:** Are there daily habits you've established to encourage a positive mindset?

**Spiritual Practices:** How do spiritual practices (prayer, worship, fasting) influence your mental state?

**Self-Assessment on Cleansing the Mind for a Child:**

**Thought Sharing:** How often does your child share their thoughts or feelings with you?

**Media Exposure:** What type of content does your child engage with? Is it age-appropriate and positive?

**Daily Reflection:** Do you have a routine where your child reflects on their day, discussing highs and lows?

**Scripture Engagement:** How do you incorporate spiritual teachings or scriptures into your child's life?

**Peer Influence:** Are there friends or peers who consistently influence your child either positively or negatively?

**Expression Outlets:** Does your child have outlets to express their feelings, like drawing, journaling, or speaking?

**Mindful Activities:** Are there activities you do with your child to promote mindfulness, like breathing exercises or guided imagery?

**Self-Perception:** How does your child perceive themselves? Do they express feelings of worthiness and self-love?

**Coping Mechanisms:** How does your child cope with stress or negative emotions?

**Guidance and Support:** How do you guide your child in navigating negative or confusing thoughts?


For both adults and children, these assessments can serve as a reflective tool to gauge where they currently stand in their journey of mind purification. Regular self-checks can help identify areas that may need attention or adjustment, fostering a continuous journey toward mental and spiritual wellness.

# Chapter 4: Nurturing the Spirit

The essence of humanity extends beyond the tangible body and mind, delving into the profound realms of the spirit and soul. In the biblical context, while closely linked, the spirit and soul have nuanced differences.

## The Distinction Between Spirit and Soul in the Bible:

The Bible presents the human being as a triune entity: body, soul, and spirit. Hebrews 4:12 states, "For the word of God is alive and active. Sharper than any double-edged sword, it penetrates even to dividing soul and spirit, joints and marrow; it judges the thoughts and attitudes of the heart." Here, the soul often embodies our emotions, will, and consciousness, whereas the spirit is the divine breath, the God-given essence that connects us directly with the Divine.

## How to Keep the Spirit Aligned with God's Purpose:

Aligning the spirit with God's purpose requires conscious effort, a consistent seeking of God's presence, and surrendering to His will. Through practices like reading and meditating on scriptures, participating in sacraments, and surrounding oneself with a faith-filled community, the spirit is nurtured and strengthened. Galatians 5:25 reminds us, "Since we live by the Spirit, let us keep in step with the Spirit."

## The Power of Prayer, Worship, and Communion with God:

Prayer serves as the direct line of communication with God, allowing for expression, supplication, and gratitude. Worship, whether done individually or collectively, acknowledges God's sovereignty, drawing the spirit into a state of reverence. Acts of communion, be it through the Eucharist or quiet moments of reflection, remind us of the covenant relationship with God and Jesus' sacrifice.

## Ministerial and Holistic Approach with a Human Behaviorist Perspective:

From a ministerial viewpoint, nurturing the spirit is central to spiritual growth. It involves active participation in religious sacraments, regular church attendance, and fostering a personal relationship with God. Holistically, practices such as deep meditation, spiritual retreats, and even certain therapeutic modalities can help connect with the spirit. Behaviorists might emphasize the environment's role in influencing spiritual practices, suggesting that creating conducive surroundings and routines can reinforce spiritual habits and behaviors.

**In a Child's Language:**

Imagine your spirit is like a little light inside of you. The Bible says we have a body, which is like the lampshade, and we have feelings and thoughts, which are like the switch. But the spirit? It's the bright light that shines out when we connect with God. Just like a plant needs sunlight and water to grow, our spirit needs special care too. Reading stories from the Bible, talking to God through prayer, singing songs about Him, and spending time thinking about God are like giving our inner light all the good stuff it needs to shine bright and strong. And guess what? When our light is shining brightly, it helps us make good choices, be kinder, and feel happier.

In essence, the journey of nurturing the spirit is a lifelong endeavor, one that involves continuous connection, reflection, and alignment with God's will. Whether you're an adult or a child, the pursuit of a vibrant spirit, closely aligned with the Divine, offers a life enriched with purpose, joy, and eternal promise.

**Self-Assessment on Nurturing the Spirit for Different Groups:**

**For Adults:**

**Daily Practices:** How often do you engage in spiritual practices such as prayer, meditation, or reading scriptures?

**Community Engagement:** Are you part of a spiritual or religious community? How actively do you participate?

**Life Alignment:** Do you feel your daily life aligns with your spiritual beliefs and values?

**Obstacles:** What challenges or distractions do you face in nurturing your spirit?

**Growth:** Are there spiritual disciplines or practices you wish to incorporate into your life?

**For Children:**

**Understanding:** How would you describe God or a higher power?

**Daily Habits:** Do you have a routine of praying or thanking God before meals or bedtime?

**Questions:** What questions do you have about God, spirituality, or the world around you?

**Feelings:** How do you feel when you think about God or attend religious gatherings?

**Stories:** What's your favorite story or lesson from religious texts or teachings?

**For Families:**

**Shared Practices:** As a family, how often do you engage in shared spiritual practices, such as praying or attending services together?

**Spiritual Conversations:** How frequently do you discuss spiritual topics or values at home?

**Family Values:** Are your family values clearly defined and understood by all members? How do they align with your spiritual beliefs?

**Support:** How do you support each family member in their individual spiritual journey?

**Traditions:** Are there family traditions related to your faith or spirituality? Would you like to start any new ones?

### For People with Disabilities:

**Accessibility:** Do you have access to spiritual or religious communities that accommodate and understand your needs?

**Personal Connection:** How do you personally connect with your spiritual side? Are there practices that you find particularly meaningful or comforting?

**Support:** Are there individuals or groups that support you in your spiritual journey?

**Challenges:** What unique challenges do you face in nurturing your spirit because of your disability?

**Adaptations:** Are there adaptations or modifications you've made to traditional spiritual practices to suit your needs?

For each group, the assessment serves as a reflective tool, offering insight into the current state of their spiritual journey. It's a chance to understand where they currently stand, what challenges they face, and what steps might be necessary for growth and deeper connection. Regular reflection and assessment can pave the way for a richer, more fulfilling spiritual life.

# Chapter 5: The Soul's Sanctity

The soul is a profound concept, often perceived as the eternal and true self that transcends the limitations of our mortal bodies. Its significance in religious and spiritual contexts cannot be overstated.

**Understanding the Immortal Soul:**

In various religious beliefs, the soul is viewed as immortal, continuing its existence even after the death of the physical body. The Bible presents the soul as the very essence of life, given by God and returning to Him upon death. This eternal nature underscores the soul's profound worth and the imperative to tend to its well-being.

**Repentance, Confession, and Redemption: Keeping the Soul Pure:**

The spiritual journey is seldom without missteps. However, the Bible offers a path to realign and cleanse the soul: repentance and confession. Acts 3:19 says, "Repent, then, and turn to God, so that your sins may be wiped out." True repentance is a heartfelt remorse for one's wrongs, followed by a genuine effort to change. Confession, whether private to God or shared with trusted members of a faith community, brings darkness into light, initiating healing. Redemption, brought about by Christ's sacrifice, reaffirms that no soul is beyond saving, emphasizing God's boundless mercy and love.

## The Significance of the Soul in the Overall Well-Being of a Believer:

The soul's health deeply impacts a believer's overall well-being. A nurtured soul radiates joy, peace, and purpose, while a neglected one might manifest discontent, despair, or aimlessness. Just as one would tend to physical ailments, the soul requires care, reflection, and connection with the Divine to flourish.

## Ministerial and Holistic Approach with a Human Behaviorist Perspective:

From a ministerial standpoint, the soul's sanctity is paramount. Leaders guide believers through sacraments, teachings, and community support, ensuring each soul finds its path to God. Holistically, practitioners might advocate for practices like deep introspection, mindfulness, and even therapeutic modalities that foster soulful connections. A behaviorist might stress the environmental stimuli affecting the soul's state, suggesting habits, routines, and surroundings that nurture and protect its sanctity.

## In a Child's Language:

Imagine the soul as a special, glowing heart inside of you. This glowing heart is very, very special because it never gets old or tired; it's always there, even when our bodies grow old. Sometimes, we might do things that put a little cloud over our glowing heart, like when we're naughty or mean. But guess what? When we say sorry and really mean it, that cloud goes away, and our glowing heart shines bright again! It's essential to keep our special heart happy by doing good things, being kind, and talking to God because when it's happy, we feel our very best.

In essence, the soul is the eternal core of our being, deserving utmost reverence and care. By intertwining biblical teachings with holistic practices and behavioral insights, believers of all ages can navigate the journey of maintaining their soul's sanctity in a multifaceted world.

## Self-Assessment on Family's Participation in Soul Sanctity

This assessment is designed to help families reflect on their collective and individual journeys in nurturing the soul's sanctity. The questions are framed to encompass various family members, recognizing the importance of inclusivity.

## General Family Assessment:

How does your family collectively practice spiritual or religious rituals that contribute to soul sanctity?

Are there shared values or beliefs that guide your family's decisions and actions?

How does your family create an environment that nurtures the soul?

## For Adults:

How do you ensure your actions and decisions align with the sanctity of your soul?

What practices or rituals do you personally undertake to nurture your soul?

How do you support other family members, especially children, in understanding and respecting the soul's sanctity?

**For Children:**

How do you feel about the family's spiritual or religious practices? Are there parts you especially like or don't understand?

How do you personally connect with the idea of having a special, glowing heart (soul) inside you?

Are there questions or things you'd like to explore more about the soul?

**For Persons with Disabilities:**

Are the family's spiritual or religious practices accessible and inclusive to you? If not, what modifications would help?

How do you personally connect with and nurture your soul? Are there practices that resonate with you particularly?

How can the family better support your unique journey in understanding and cherishing the soul's sanctity?

**For Different Cultures within the Family:**

How does your cultural background influence your understanding and practices concerning the soul's sanctity?

Are there specific rituals, teachings, or values from your culture that you've integrated into the family's spiritual journey?

How does the family ensure that various cultural perspectives on the soul are acknowledged and celebrated?

**Reflection:** After answering these questions, families can discuss their responses together. This provides a space for open dialogue, ensuring that each member's journey is acknowledged and supported. Such discussions can be powerful in strengthening bonds, understanding individual paths, and ensuring that the family grows collectively in their pursuit of soul sanctity.

# Chapter 6: The Armor of God

The world we navigate is not just of the seen but the unseen, not just of the tangible but the spiritual. Ephesians 6:10-18 provides a powerful metaphor for the spiritual defenses' believers must don: the Armor of God. This armor isn't physical; it's a collection of spiritual strengths and virtues that shield us from spiritual adversaries.

## Ephesians 6:10-18: Breaking Down the Armor

**Belt of Truth:** Just as a belt holds other pieces of armor in place, truth grounds us. It represents sincerity, honesty, and understanding God's word. By upholding truth, believers can stand firm against deceit and falsehood.

**Breastplate of Righteousness:** The breastplate protects the heart and vital organs, symbolizing moral integrity and upright behavior. Righteous living guards one's heart against the corrupting influences of the world.

**Feet Fitted with Readiness:** Derived from the Gospel of Peace, this signifies the importance of spreading God's message of love and peace. It also means being ready and grounded in faith, able to stand firm against challenges.

**Shield of Faith:** Faith is our primary defense against the doubts, fears, and negative influences that can assail us. Like a shield, faith can deflect these spiritual attacks if we hold it up and trust in God.

**Helmet of Salvation:** The helmet, which safeguards the mind, signifies the believer's salvation and assurance in Christ. With this assurance, believers can face spiritual battles without fear.

**Sword of the Spirit:** The only offensive weapon in this armor, it represents God's word. Just as a sword can pierce, the truths of the Bible can penetrate hearts and confront evil.

## Utilizing the Armor in Daily Life

From a ministerial viewpoint, the Armor of God is essential for spiritual growth and defense against the temptations and challenges of life. Leaders emphasize regular Bible study, prayer, and community involvement as ways to strengthen and maintain this armor.

Holistically, the armor can be seen as an integration of spiritual beliefs with daily habits and behaviors. It's about aligning actions with values, grounding oneself in foundational truths, and actively practicing faith.

Behaviorists might view the armor as positive reinforcements. Upholding truth, living righteously, and grounding oneself in faith can lead to beneficial outcomes, reinforcing these behaviors. Negative stimuli or consequences can be minimized or counteracted when one is "armored" correctly.

**In a Child's Language:**

Imagine you're a brave knight! You have special armor that helps keep you safe from things that might try to hurt you. But this isn't just any armor; it's super special:

- A belt that helps you always tell the truth.
- A big chest piece that helps you do good things and make right choices.
- Shoes that make you ready to spread love and happiness.
- A big shield, which is your belief in God that keeps you safe.
- A helmet that reminds you always of God's love and how He saved us.
- And a shiny sword, which is like the stories and lessons from the Bible, helping you stand strong.

So, whenever things get tough or scary, remember you're a knight with God's special armor, and nothing can beat that!

In essence, the Armor of God is not about warfare in the traditional sense. It's about equipping oneself spiritually to navigate the challenges of life with faith, truth, and righteousness, irrespective of age or understanding.

## Self-Assessment on the Armor of God for Families, Persons with Disabilities, and Multiple Cultures

Understanding and embracing the Armor of God is essential for spiritual growth. This self-assessment is tailored to ensure inclusivity, catering to the diverse needs of families, individuals with disabilities, and those from various cultural backgrounds.

### General Family Assessment:

How do we, as a family, currently understand and relate to the Armor of God?

How can we better integrate the teachings of the Armor of God into our daily lives?

Are there family activities or rituals that can help us collectively strengthen each piece of the armor?

### For Persons with Disabilities:

Are there aspects of the Armor of God that resonate particularly with your personal experiences or challenges?

How can teachings or practices related to the Armor of God be made more accessible or relevant to you?

What support or modifications would you appreciate from the family to better understand and embody the Armor of God?

### For Different Cultures within the Family:

Are there similarities or parallels in your cultural or spiritual background to the Armor of God?

How can the family incorporate diverse cultural perspectives into our understanding of the Armor of God?

Are there unique rituals, stories, or teachings from your culture that can enhance our collective appreciation of the Armor of God?

**Reflection & Action Points:**

Which piece of the Armor do we feel strongest in, and which requires more attention?

Are there specific family members who might offer unique insights or strengths concerning a particular piece of the Armor?

How can we ensure that our family environment remains open, respectful, and inclusive when discussing and reflecting on the Armor of God?

The essence of this assessment is to foster open dialogue, understanding, and collective growth. Through shared reflections and mutual support, families can deepen their connection to the Armor of God, considering the unique perspectives and needs of each member.

# Chapter 7: Discipline and Discipleship

Every believer's journey is marked by peaks of spiritual euphoria and valleys of doubt and temptation. In navigating this terrain, discipline becomes not just a virtue but a necessity. Being a disciple, after all, is rooted in discipline. This discipline is not about strict rules but about training oneself to align more closely with God's will.

## The Centrality of Discipline

The Bible emphasizes discipline as a central component of a believer's growth. Without it, one is susceptible to the winds of worldly distractions and temptations. Discipline helps mold believers into true disciples, those who not only follow but embody Christ's teachings.

## Biblical Figures of Self-control, Perseverance, and Resilience:

**Joseph:** A story of immense self-control, he resisted Potipar's wife's advances, choosing righteousness over immediate pleasure. His perseverance was further demonstrated when he was unjustly imprisoned, maintaining his faith even in confinement. And his resilience? It shone when he rose to prominence in Egypt, not through bitterness but through wisdom and leadership.

**Job:** Perhaps no other figure embodies perseverance and resilience like Job. Despite losing nearly everything—family, wealth, health—he refused to curse God. His story is a testament to unwavering faith amid profound suffering.

**Paul:** From persecuting Christians to becoming one of Christianity's most influential apostles, Paul's journey was one of self-control (especially in spreading the Gospel), perseverance (in his missionary journeys), and resilience (facing numerous adversities for his faith).

## Navigating Life's Challenges

Temptations and distractions are not modern phenomena; they have always existed. However, with today's hyper-connected world, they've amplified. Here, the ministerial perspective would emphasize grounding oneself in Scripture, community, and regular worship.

From a holistic viewpoint, it's about balance. Balancing spiritual practices with physical well-being, mental health, and emotional self-awareness can bolster one's discipline.

The behaviorist perspective focuses on developing habits. Repetitive positive behaviors, like regular prayer or Bible study, can reinforce spiritual discipline, while also offering rewards in terms of inner peace and community connection.

**In a Child's Language:**

Imagine you're training to become a superhero! To be the best superhero, you need to practice, just like how athletes train for big races. The Bible tells us stories of some super cool heroes who trained their hearts and minds to be strong and do good:

**Joseph** was like a superhero who said "No" to bad things, even when it was tough.

**Job** was super strong, not giving up even when everything went wrong.

**Paul** traveled far and wide, telling everyone about Jesus, and he never gave up, no matter how tough things got.

So, remember, to be a spiritual superhero, practice makes perfect! Train your heart, mind, and spirit to be strong, kind, and full of love.

In essence, discipline is the path that molds believers into true disciples. It's not about avoiding the world but engaging with it fully, armored with faith and a heart aligned with God's purpose.

## Self-Assessment on Becoming More Disciplined and Embracing Discipleship

This self-assessment is designed to encourage introspection and reflection on one's journey towards discipline and discipleship, catering to the diverse needs of families, children, individuals with disabilities, and those from various spiritual backgrounds.

### For Adults:

How would you rate your current level of spiritual discipline? What practices are you consistently maintaining?

Are there areas in your life where you struggle with self-control or perseverance?

How do you seek spiritual guidance or support when faced with worldly distractions or temptations?

### For Children:

Can you think of a time when you had to be really patient or say 'no' to something you wanted right away?

What makes you feel close to God or your spiritual beliefs?

Are there stories or heroes from the Bible or other spiritual teachings that inspire you to be strong and kind?

### For Families:

How does our family currently foster discipline and discipleship? Are there rituals or practices we can adopt to strengthen this?

How do we support one another during challenging times or when one of us feels spiritually distant?

Are there specific cultural or spiritual teachings that our family uniquely holds? How can we celebrate and integrate them into our collective spiritual journey?

**For Persons with Disabilities:**

How accessible and inclusive do you find spiritual teachings and practices to be for your specific needs?

Are there particular challenges or experiences related to your disability that influence your spiritual journey or discipline?

How can the family or community better support your spiritual growth and understanding?

**For Families with Mixed Spiritual Cultures:**

How do we respect and honor the diverse spiritual backgrounds within our family?

Are there shared values or teachings that cross our spiritual cultures? How can we emphasize these in our daily lives?

How can we ensure that each family member feels seen, understood, and celebrated in their unique spiritual journey?

**Reflection & Action Points:**

What are our strengths as individuals and as a family in practicing discipline and discipleship?

Are there resources, communities, or practices we can explore to further nurture our spiritual discipline?

How can we regularly check-in with each other, ensuring open communication and mutual support in our spiritual journeys?

Using this assessment, families can open the floor for inclusive and respectful discussions about discipline and discipleship. The goal is to create an environment where every family member, irrespective of age, ability, or spiritual background, feels supported and empowered in their spiritual journey.

# Chapter 8: The Community's Role

One cannot navigate the journey of faith in isolation. The biblical narrative places significant emphasis on the role of the community—be it the Israelites in the Old Testament or the early Christian church in the New Testament. Within these communities, believers find strength, support, and shared purpose.

## The Church and the Community

In the New Testament, the church isn't just a physical structure but a body of believers. Just as different parts of the body serve unique functions, each member of the community has a distinct role to play. Their collective strength and unity are evident in the Acts of the Apostles, where believers met regularly, pooling resources, breaking bread, and ensuring no one was in need.

## Accountability, Fellowship, and Collective Worship

Believers encourage and correct each other in love. Biblical characters like Nathan exemplify accountability; he bravely confronted King David over his sin with Bathsheba. Similarly, Paul and Barnabas shared a fellowship, supporting each other in their missionary endeavors but also having disagreements, demonstrating that community involves both harmony and constructive friction.

Collective worship, as seen in the early church's gatherings, creates a shared spiritual experience. Singing hymns, studying scriptures, and partaking in the Lord's Supper not only nurtures individual souls but also fortifies the collective spirit.

## Spiritual Mentorship and Guidance

Timothy's relationship with Paul is a classic example of spiritual mentorship. Paul nurtured Timothy, guiding him in his ministry and providing wisdom. This relationship underscores the importance of having seasoned believers guiding newer ones, ensuring the faith's transmission across generations.

## A Holistic and Behaviorist Perspective

From a holistic view, the community offers emotional, psychological, and spiritual support. Being part of a community can provide a sense of belonging, reduce feelings of isolation, and contribute to overall well-being.

Behaviorists would stress the positive reinforcement provided by a community. When one witnesses others leading a disciplined life, it serves as a motivation. The regularity of communal activities, like weekly services or Bible studies, helps instill positive habits in believers.

## In a Child's Language:

Imagine a puzzle. Each piece is unique, but when they come together, they create a beautiful picture. The church or believers' community is like that puzzle. Every person, including you, is an essential piece.

Remember the story of David and his friend Nathan? Nathan was like a kind friend who told David when he was making a mistake, just like how our friends in our community help and guide us. And just like Paul helped Timothy learn and grow, there are older people in our community who teach us and help us be the best we can be.

Being part of this big puzzle or family is fun! We sing together, learn together, and help each other, just like a big, loving family.

In essence, the believers' community, enriched by diverse members and unified in purpose, plays a pivotal role in nurturing individual spiritual journeys, emphasizing the idea that while faith is personal, the journey of belief is collective.

## Self-Assessment on Involvement in the Community's Role

Engaging in a community of believers enriches the spiritual journey for individuals and families. This self-assessment offers a deep dive into your current involvement and suggests areas for growth within the community.

### For Individuals:

How active are you in your spiritual community? In what areas do you participate?

Are there mentors or leaders within the community from whom you seek guidance?

How do you offer your skills or talents for the benefit of the community?

Are there community activities or groups you've considered joining but haven't? What holds you back?

How does the community support your personal spiritual growth? Are there areas where you feel unfulfilled or disconnected?

### For Families:

As a family, how do we prioritize involvement in our spiritual community?

Are there family-oriented community activities we actively participate in? Are there any we wish to explore?

How do we encourage each other to take on roles or responsibilities within the community?

Do we engage in discussions about our community experiences at home? How can we create more space for these conversations?

Are there families within the community with whom we can foster stronger relationships?

**For Children:**

What activities or groups are you involved in at church or within the spiritual community? Which ones do you enjoy the most?

Are there elders or mentors you look up to or learn from in the community?

Do you have friends in the community? How do they help you in your spiritual journey?

Are there activities or roles you'd like to try or be more involved in?

How does being a part of this community make you feel? Are there moments when you feel proud or times you feel left out?

**Reflection & Action Points:**

What are our individual and collective strengths in engaging with our spiritual community?

Which areas or activities within the community resonate with our spiritual goals? Are there new avenues we'd like to explore?

How can we set actionable steps to deepen our involvement and engagement in the community?

Are there members of the community we can reach out to for mentorship, guidance, or collaboration?

How do we ensure that every family member feels supported, seen, and valued in their community interactions?

This self-assessment is designed to kindle introspection and proactive engagement with the spiritual community. It fosters an environment of shared responsibility and mutual growth, ensuring that individuals and families find meaningful ways to connect, contribute, and flourish within their spiritual communities.

# Chapter 9: Celebrating Sabbaths and Festivals

The rhythm of rest and celebration has been woven into the fabric of Judeo-Christian tradition from the very beginning. Both the sabbath and religious festivals are divine mandates, not just as rituals, but as vital components of spiritual and physical health.

## Role of Rest and Celebration

Rest is not merely cessation from labor; it's a deep rejuvenation. The Creation account in Genesis underscores this, where after six days of work, God rested on the seventh, sanctifying it. This rest serves multiple purposes - it's a time of reflection, gratitude, and renewal, offering a balance to the toil and challenges faced during the week.

Celebrations, on the other hand, are collective reminders of God's love, grace, and power. Festivals like Passover, which commemorates the Israelites' liberation from Egypt, or the Feast of Tabernacles, a time to recall the divine guidance during their wilderness journey, are not just historical markers but spiritual reorientations.

## Observing Sabbaths

For adults, the sabbath could be a day free from work-related stresses, a time to delve deeper into scriptures, pray, meditate, and engage with family and community. For children, it's an opportunity to understand the value of gratitude and reflection. Even in diverse backgrounds, the essence of sabbath can resonate: a universally understood need for rest and rejuvenation.

Persons with disabilities, too, can find unique ways to observe the sabbath. It could be through specialized spiritual programs, assistive worship sessions, or simply in the quiet embrace of God's love in a setting that comforts them.

## Celebrating Festivals

God's festivals are joyous occasions, serving as waypoints on the believer's journey. Adults can recount stories of God's deliverance and promises, ensuring that they're passed down. For children, these festivals can be a mix of awe (imagining the parting of the Red Sea during Passover) and joy (dwelling in makeshift huts during the Feast of Tabernacles).

For individuals from diverse backgrounds, these festivals can be intersections of culture and faith. Imagine a Passover Seder where stories of liberation from multiple cultures are shared, or a Pentecost celebration with prayers in various languages, reflecting the Holy Spirit's gift of tongues.

For persons with disabilities, celebrations can be adapted to ensure inclusivity. This could be through tactile experiences, visual stories, or auditory aids, ensuring that the joy and lessons of the festivals are accessible to all.

In essence, sabbaths and festivals are God's gift to His people. They're not just dates on a calendar but soulful pauses, allowing believers of all backgrounds and abilities to reflect, rejoice, and reenergize in their spiritual journey. They remind us of the balance between work and rest, sorrow and joy, and the ever-present love and power of the Divine in our lives.

## Self-Assessment on Celebrating Sabbaths and Festivals

Taking time for introspection can help you gauge your engagement with and understanding of the Sabbaths and festivals. This self-assessment offers a starting point for such reflection.

### Understanding and Observance:

How do you currently observe the Sabbath? Is it a day of rest, reflection, or a combination of both?

Which biblical festivals are you familiar with, and how do you celebrate them?

Are there specific aspects of these festivals that resonate deeply with you? Why?

How does observing the Sabbath and festivals affect your spiritual and emotional well-being?

### Engaging with Family and Community:

How does your family observe the Sabbath and participate in festivals? Are there family traditions associated with them?

How involved are you in communal celebrations of these festivals?

Are there community resources or gatherings you can tap into for a richer celebration and understanding of these occasions?

### Inclusivity and Adaptability:

If you have children, how do you make the stories and traditions of the Sabbath and festivals relevant and engaging for them?

For those from diverse backgrounds: Are there cultural traditions or festivals that you can integrate with biblical ones for a richer experience?

If you or someone in your family has a disability, how have you adapted the celebrations to be more inclusive and accessible?

**Deepening Understanding:**

Are there festivals mentioned in the Bible that you aren't familiar with or don't currently observe? Would you be interested in learning more about them?

How can you deepen your understanding of the significance behind each festival?

Are there books, courses, or community classes available that might enhance your appreciation and observance of these sacred times?

**Reflection & Action Points:**

Which areas of Sabbath observance and festival celebration feel most fulfilling to you? Which areas might need more attention or enrichment?

Can you identify any actionable steps to deepen your engagement with these sacred times?

How can you ensure that these celebrations are inclusive and resonate with all family members, regardless of age, background, or ability?

Engaging in this self-assessment can help you approach Sabbaths and festivals with renewed intention. These sacred times are not just ritualistic observances but profound opportunities for connection, reflection, and celebration. By taking time to evaluate and adapt your practices, you can cultivate a deeper, more personal relationship with these divine gifts.

# Chapter 10: The Coming of Christ

In Christian theology, the Second Coming of Christ signifies the anticipated return of Jesus to Earth. This profound event is a central pillar of the faith, with ramifications not only for the spiritual realm but also for how believers lead their daily lives.

## Living in Anticipation of Christ's Return

Throughout the New Testament, believers are urged to live in active anticipation of Christ's return. The early disciples and apostles lived with an acute sense of this impending event. Paul, for instance, consistently encouraged churches to live righteously, exemplifying his own life of sacrifice and devotion. The Thessalonians were so eager for the return that Paul had to remind them of their earthly responsibilities while they waited (1 Thessalonians 4:13-18).

Similarly, the apostle Peter, in his letters, stressed the importance of leading a life of holiness and godliness, "looking forward and hastening the coming of the day of God" (2 Peter 3:12).

From a ministerial perspective, living in anticipation means nurturing a community that's rooted in faith, hope, and love. It's about grounding practices and teachings in the sure hope of Christ's return, ensuring that the community is spiritually vigilant and robust.

In terms of human behavior, this anticipation can act as a motivational tool. The promise of Christ's return can inspire individuals to assess their actions, realigning them with the values and teachings of the faith. Just as the knowledge of an impending guest can spur one to clean and prepare their home, so does the anticipation of Christ's return urge believers to cleanse their hearts and minds.

**For Children:** Think of awaiting Christ's return as waiting for a most special guest, someone you deeply love and respect. Imagine preparing your room for this guest, cleaning every nook and corner. In the same way, we prepare our hearts and lives for Jesus, making sure our actions and thoughts are kind, loving, and true.

## Signs, Preparation, and Rewards

The Bible speaks of various signs that would precede Christ's return, including moral decay, natural calamities, and widespread apostasy (Matthew 24, 2 Timothy 3). However, rather than becoming overly focused on these signs, believers are called to prepare by keeping their "temples" clean – their bodies, minds, spirits, and souls.

This preparation is more than mere ritual; it's about genuine repentance, steadfast faith, and tangible love towards God and fellow humans. The reward for such preparation is eternal – the promise of everlasting life with Christ, an inheritance that is "imperishable, undefiled, and unfading" (1 Peter 1:4).

## The Final Judgement

The Second Coming culminates in the Final Judgement, where every individual's life will be assessed. As believers, our responsibilities are two-fold: to ensure our walk aligns with Christ's teachings and to evangelize, bringing others into the fold. The Parable of the Ten Virgins (Matthew 25:1-13) is a stark reminder to always be prepared, to keep our lamps trimmed and burning.

In essence, the Second Coming is not a mere future event to passively await. It's a catalyst, inspiring believers from all walks of life to live with purpose, purity, and passion, continually realigning with the path Jesus set before us.

## Self-Assessment on Preparing for the Coming of Christ

Engaging in introspection and reflection about one's readiness for the coming of Christ is crucial for deepening one's faith. The following self-assessment offers questions to guide you and your family members, irrespective of age, abilities, or cultural backgrounds, in this reflection.

### Personal Preparedness:

How often do you reflect on your personal relationship with Christ?

Are there areas in your life that need realignment with the teachings of Jesus?

How do you nurture your spiritual growth? Are there practices or rituals you engage in regularly?

### Family Dynamics:

How do you instill the values and teachings of Jesus in your children?

Are there family rituals or practices you uphold to reinforce the anticipation of Christ's return?

How do you address and reconcile differing religious or spiritual views within your family?

**For Children:**

Do your children know about the Second Coming? How do you explain it to them in a way that's hopeful and not fear-inducing?

How do you ensure your children's spiritual nourishment aligns with the values of awaiting Christ's return?

**Inclusivity for Persons with Disabilities:**

How do you make spiritual teachings and practices accessible for family members with disabilities?

Are there specialized resources or communities you're part of that focus on inclusivity in spiritual practices?

**Engaging with Diverse Cultures & Beliefs:**

For families with mixed religious or cultural backgrounds: How do you respect and incorporate different beliefs while also teaching about the coming of Christ?

How do you approach conversations with family members who have different religious beliefs, ensuring mutual respect and understanding?

**Community Engagement:**

How involved are you in your religious community? Does this engagement help reinforce your readiness for the Second Coming?

Are there community events or practices that focus on preparing for Christ's return that you participate in?

**Continuous Learning & Growth:**

Are there books, scriptures, or courses you plan to explore to deepen your understanding of the Second Coming?

How do you keep updated with theological interpretations or teachings about the coming of Christ?

**Reflection & Action Points:**

Which areas of your readiness for the coming of Christ feel solid? Where might there be room for growth?

Can you identify any actionable steps or practices to enhance your preparation and that of your family?

How can you foster an environment of continuous learning and anticipation within your family regarding this central tenet of faith?

By actively engaging in this assessment, you reinforce your commitment and readiness for Christ's return. It also ensures that all family members, regardless of their age, background, or abilities, are included in this spiritual journey.

## Conclusion

The journey of discipleship is not a mere adherence to rituals or practices; it is an all-encompassing commitment that touches every facet of a believer's life. In the intricate tapestry of our existence, the threads of body, mind, spirit, and soul are intertwined, and each plays a pivotal role in our spiritual voyage.

## Holistic Purity:

From a biblical perspective, the call to maintain purity is not just limited to one's physical being. It extends to our thoughts, emotions, intentions, and the very essence of our soul. True purity emerges from a synergy of all these components. Just as a temple is revered and maintained with utmost devotion, so should we honor and care for our 'temples' - ensuring that our bodies are treated with respect, our minds are filled with virtuous thoughts, our spirits remain aligned with God's purpose, and our souls are always yearning for divine connection.

## Reflections on Discipleship:

The journey of discipleship is filled with mountains and valleys. There are moments of profound spiritual insights, and there are times of doubt and despair. Yet, each step, whether forward or seemingly backward, contributes to our spiritual growth. Reflecting on personal experiences, it becomes evident that trials often precede triumphs and that faith is solidified not just in moments of clarity, but also in moments of questioning. The stories of biblical characters, from Moses to Mary and from Paul to Peter, serve as testaments to this dynamic journey of faith. They had their moments of doubt, but their perseverance and reliance on God led them to spiritual heights.

## A Call to Steadfastness:

In a world teeming with distractions, staying steadfast in one's walk with God can be challenging. Yet, the rewards of such steadfastness are eternal. Believers are encouraged to anchor themselves in the Word, to find solace in prayer, to draw strength from their community, and to continually seek God's guidance. As the anticipation of Christ's return provides a focal point, it's essential to remember the daily journey and the continuous commitment to keeping our 'temples' pure and our hearts aligned with God.

In essence, the holistic approach to maintaining purity and the emphasis on the intertwined nature of body, mind, spirit, and soul underscores the beauty and depth of the Christian faith. As believers continue their journey, may they do so with hope, resilience, and an unwavering faith in the promises of God.

## Appendix

### A list of Bible verses for meditation and reflection

**Psalm 46:10** - "Be still, and know that I am God; I will be exalted among the nations, I will be exalted in the earth."

**Joshua 1:8** - "Keep this Book of the Law always on your lips; meditate on it day and night, so that you may be careful to do everything written in it. Then you will be prosperous and successful."

**Philippians 4:8** - "Finally, brothers and sisters, whatever is true, whatever is noble, whatever is right, whatever is pure, whatever is lovely, whatever is admirable—if anything is excellent or praiseworthy—think about such things."

**Matthew 11:28** - "Come to me, all you who are weary and burdened, and I will give you rest."

**Psalm 1:1-3** - "Blessed is the one... whose delight is in the law of the LORD, and who meditates on his law day and night. That person is like a tree planted by streams of water, which yields its fruit in season and whose leaf does not wither—whatever they do prospers."

**Romans 12:2** - "Do not conform to the pattern of this world, but be transformed by the renewing of your mind. Then you will be able to test and approve what God's will is—his good, pleasing and perfect will."

**Psalm 119:15-16** - "I meditate on your precepts and consider your ways. I delight in your decrees; I will not neglect your word."

**Colossians 3:2** - "Set your minds on things above, not on earthly things."

**Jeremiah 29:11** - "For I know the plans I have for you, declares the LORD, plans for welfare and not for evil, to give you a future and hope."

**Isaiah 26:3** - "You will keep in perfect peace those whose minds are steadfast, because they trust in you."

**Proverbs 3:5-6** - "Trust in the LORD with all your heart and lean not on your own understanding; in all your ways submit to him, and he will make your paths straight."

**2 Timothy 1:7** - "For God has not given us a spirit of fear, but of power and of love and of a sound mind."

**Psalm 19:14** - "May the words of my mouth and the meditation of my heart be pleasing in your sight, O LORD, my Rock and my Redeemer."

**1 Peter 5:7** - "Cast all your anxiety on him because he cares for you."

**John 15:5** - "I am the vine; you are the branches. If you remain in me and I in you, you will bear much fruit; apart from me you can do nothing."

Each of these verses offers profound wisdom and can be a starting point for deeper reflection and understanding. Whether you're seeking guidance, peace, encouragement, or simply want to draw closer to God, meditating on these scriptures can be a transformative experience.


**Suggested reading for further study**

**Biblical Texts:**

**"The Book of Psalms"** - Offers a deep well of prayers, laments, praises, and reflections.

**"The Sermon on the Mount"** (**Matthew 5-7**) - Jesus' teachings on righteous living and spiritual growth.

"The Letters of Paul" - Particularly Romans, Corinthians, Galatians, and Philippians. They delve into various aspects of Christian living and spiritual discipline.

**Books by Christian Authors:**

"The Cost of Discipleship" by Dietrich Bonhoeffer - A profound look at the demands and rewards of Christian discipleship.

"The Pursuit of Holiness" by Jerry Bridges - A guide on how to lead a life of sanctification and purity.

"The Spirit of the Disciplines" by Dallas Willard - An exploration of spiritual disciplines that can lead to a transformed life.

"Celebration of Discipline" by Richard Foster - Details various spiritual disciplines that can deepen one's relationship with God.

"Mere Christianity" by C.S. Lewis - A classic text on Christian belief and practice.

"Boundaries" by Dr. Henry Cloud & Dr. John Townsend - A guide to understanding and setting healthy boundaries from a Christian perspective.

**For a Behavioral Perspective:**

"The Road Less Traveled" by M. Scott Peck - Merges psychological insights with spiritual wisdom.

"Switch: How to Change Things When Change Is Hard" by Chip Heath & Dan Heath - A look at human behavior and how to cultivate positive change.

**For Families and Children:**

"Sticky Faith" by Kara Powell and Chap Clark - Focuses on building lasting faith in children and teenagers.

"The 5 Love Languages of Children" by Gary Chapman & Ross Campbell - Helps parents understand their children's unique ways of feeling loved.

**For Persons with Disabilities:**

"Beyond Suffering: Discovering the Message of Job" by Layton Talbert - A deep dive into the Book of Job and the theme of suffering.

"The Bible, Disability, and the Church: A New Vision of the People of God" by Amos Yong - A theological exploration of disability in the biblical narrative.

**For Multicultural and Interfaith Understanding:**

"Encountering God: A Spiritual Journey from Bozeman to Banaras" by Diana L. Eck - A perspective on understanding and appreciating different faith traditions.

"The Next Evangelicalism: Freeing the Church from Western Cultural Captivity" by Soong-Chan Rah - A call for a more multicultural approach to Christianity.

Remember, the journey of discipleship and understanding is a continuous process. The resources mentioned above are just starting points. Engaging in group studies, attending seminars, and participating in workshops can also provide enriched understanding and perspective.

## Activities and exercises for maintaining a clean temple

Maintaining a clean temple—referring to the purity and health of the body, mind, spirit, and soul—requires regular practices and disciplines. Here are some activities and exercises that can help you in this endeavor:

### For the Body:

**Physical Exercise:** Regular physical activity such as walking, jogging, yoga, or going to the gym. This promotes physical health and reduces stress.

**Healthy Eating:** Incorporate a balanced diet with plenty of fruits, vegetables, whole grains, lean protein, and stay hydrated.

**Fasting:** This ancient spiritual discipline can be beneficial both spiritually and physically. Always consult with a health professional before beginning.

**Adequate Sleep:** Prioritize 7-9 hours of sleep for rest and rejuvenation.

**Detox Activities:** Things like sauna sessions, body scrubs, and massages can help cleanse the body.

## For the Mind:

**Bible Study:** Regular reading, study, and meditation on the scriptures.

**Reading:** Engage in books that enhance understanding and provide spiritual or mental growth.

**Meditation and Mindfulness:** Spend time in silence, focus on breathing, and be present in the moment.

**Journaling:** Write down your thoughts, prayers, and reflections. This helps in processing emotions and gaining clarity.

**Limiting Media Consumption:** Be discerning about the information you consume. Choose uplifting and constructive content.

## For the Spirit:

**Prayer:** Set aside specific times each day for personal prayer.

**Worship:** Participate in communal worship, singing, and praising.

**Fellowship:** Engage in a spiritual community or small group where you can share, learn, and grow together.

**Service:** Volunteer your time in charitable causes and community service.

**Retreats:** Attend spiritual retreats for deeper reflection and connection with God.

## For the Soul:

**Repentance and Confession:** Regularly take time to self-reflect, repent of wrongs, and seek reconciliation.

**Practice Gratitude:** Keep a gratitude journal and list things you'r thankful for daily.

**Listen to Uplifting Music:** Music has the power to stir the soul. Choos genres and lyrics that uplift and inspire.

**Engage in Art:** Drawing, painting, or other art forms can be therapeuti for the soul.

**Nature Walks:** Spending time in nature can be refreshing for the soul.

**For Families and Community:**

**Family Devotions:** Spend time together in prayer, scripture reading and sharing.

**Workshops:** Attend workshops on spiritual growth, health, or famil bonding.

**Community Clean-Up:** Engage in activities like park clean-ups or tre planting. This physically cleans the environment and provides a sense o communal accomplishment.

Remember, these activities are not one-size-fits-all. It's essential to finc what resonates with you personally, what's sustainable in the long run and what brings you closer to maintaining a clean temple in all it aspects.

## Afterword with Jeremy B. Sims

*Jeremy B. Sims, a minister renowned for his earnest sermons, is als recognized in the holistic wellness community and among behaviorists for his unique approach to well-being. As he blends his profound theologica insights with behavioral science and holistic practices, Jeremy offers a fresh perspective on maintaining the sanctity of our "temples" in today's modern world.*

*When reflecting upon the topic of "Keeping the Temple Clean," Jeremy's own journey serves as a testament to the intertwined nature of spiritual, mental, and physical well-being. Having embarked on this journey himself, Jeremy is not just a preacher of these principles but a living example of their transformative power.*

*"In my younger days," Jeremy recalls, "I grappled with understanding the true essence of our bodies being temples. The notion seemed too abstract, distant from the tangibility's of everyday life. However, as I delved deeper into ministry and simultaneously explored the realms of human behavior and wellness, a profound revelation dawned upon me. The Bible's teachings, holistic wellness practices, and behavioral sciences all point towards one truth: the symbiotic relationship between our spiritual, mental, and physical states."*

*Jeremy emphasizes that his believer lifestyle isn't about rigid rituals or stringent rules. It's about understanding and aligning oneself with the natural laws that God has established, both spiritually and physically. "God's wisdom permeates every aspect of our existence. Whether it's the food we eat, the thoughts we nurture, or the way we connect with the divine, there's a divine blueprint waiting to be discovered and followed," Jeremy explains.*

*As a holistic wellness coach, Jeremy has helped many find balance in their lives. He often combines scriptural teachings with wellness practices, advocating for prayer and meditation, clean eating, regular exercise, and meaningful community engagement. He believes that when we treat our bodies with reverence and our minds with purity, we not only honor God but also function at our highest potential.*

*In the realm of human behavior, Jeremy's interventions often focus on breaking patterns of negative thinking, fostering resilience, and cultivating a mindset anchored in faith and optimism. "Every challenge, every setback, is an opportunity for growth and deepening our relationship with God," he often shares with his congregation and clients.*

*In conclusion, Jeremy's multidimensional approach serves as a beacon for many navigating the challenges of modern life. As believers and seekers of holistic well-being, we can all draw inspiration from his journey and insights. His life and teachings remind us that the pursuit of spiritual growth, mental clarity, and physical health is not just a personal endeavor but a divine mandate.*

# Don't miss out!

Visit the website below and you can sign up to receive emails whenever Jeremy B. Sims publishes a new book. There's no charge and no obligation.

https://books2read.com/r/B-A-CRSAB-GHRPC

**BOOKS 2 READ**

Connecting independent readers to independent writers.

Did you love *Keep That Temple Clean: A Biblical Perspective*? Then you should read *Harboring Harmony: Navigating Through Love, Freedom, and Moral Rediscovery*[1] by Jeremy B. Sims!

[2]

In "Cultivating a Space of Love and Freedom", readers embark on a transformative journey towards creating an environment that fosters love, freedom, and harmony while challenging rigid traditions that may conflict with evolving values and morals. Merging perspectives from holistic coaching, ministerial wisdom, and human behaviorist theories, the book illuminates a pathway to internal and communal harmony. Exploring themes of love, freedom, understanding, and grace, it intertwines biblical narratives and universal principles, providing practical strategies, real-life applications, and self-assessments. It delves deep into the dilemmas of holding onto traditions versus embracing

1. https://books2read.com/u/mYqLKw

2. https://books2read.com/u/mYqLKw

evolving values, illustrated by diverse cultural and personal stories from across the globe. Guiding individuals and communities towards the creation of non-judgmental spaces, the book encourages respectful dialogue and self-discovery, envisioning a future built on unity and understanding. This insightful guide is a beacon for anyone yearning to live authentically and foster a supportive and loving community, presenting a compelling narrative that advocates for a harmonious future, rooted in love and acceptance.

# Also by Jeremy B. Sims

Awakened Wellness: Are YOU Spiritually Motivated Yet?
Stop Blaming the Adversary: It's You!
From Milk to Meat: The Journey of Spiritual Maturity
Reviving Your Sacred Space: The Call for True Worshippers
Cultivating Self-Discipline: A Path to Personal and Universal Success
The Morning After
Keep That Temple Clean: A Biblical Perspective
Harboring Harmony: Navigating Through Love, Freedom, and Moral
Rediscovery